DISCARD

For the Children of East Orange Public Library!

Gingerbread Days

poems by **JOYCE CAROL THOMAS**

illustrated by **FLOYD COOPER**

JOANNA COTLER BOOKS
AN IMPRINT OF HARPERCOLLINS PUBLISHERS

Gingerbread Days
Text copyright © 1995 by Joyce Carol Thomas
Illustrations copyright © 1995 by Floyd Cooper
Printed in the U.S.A. All rights reserved.

Library of Congress Cataloging-in-Publication Data
Thomas, Joyce Carol.
  Gingerbread days / poems by Joyce Carol Thomas ; illustrated by Floyd Cooper.
      p.   cm.
  "A Joanna Cotler book."
  Summary: Poems for each month of the year celebrate the themes of family love,
individuality, and Afro-American identity.
  ISBN 0-06-023469-5. — ISBN 0-06-023472-5 (lib. bdg.)
  1. Afro-American families—Juvenile poetry.   2. Afro-Americans—Juvenile poetry.
3. Family—Juvenile poetry.   4. Children's poetry, American.   [1. Afro-Americans—
Poetry.   2. Family—Poetry.   3. American poetry.]   I. Cooper, Floyd, ill.   II. Title.
PS3570.H565G56   1995   94-19566
811'.54—dc20   CIP
                                                                              AC

Typography by Christine Kettner
1   2   3   4   5   6   7   8   9   10
❖
First Edition

For my brother
Roy Leon Haynes, M.D.
(May 27, 1936–February 1, 1979)
who enjoyed helping mothers deliver children
into the world.
Once I heard him say in a ginger voice,
"A new life. A new hope."
—JCT

To my Grand Alneeta Williams,
long Muskogee summers and hot gingerbread!
—FC

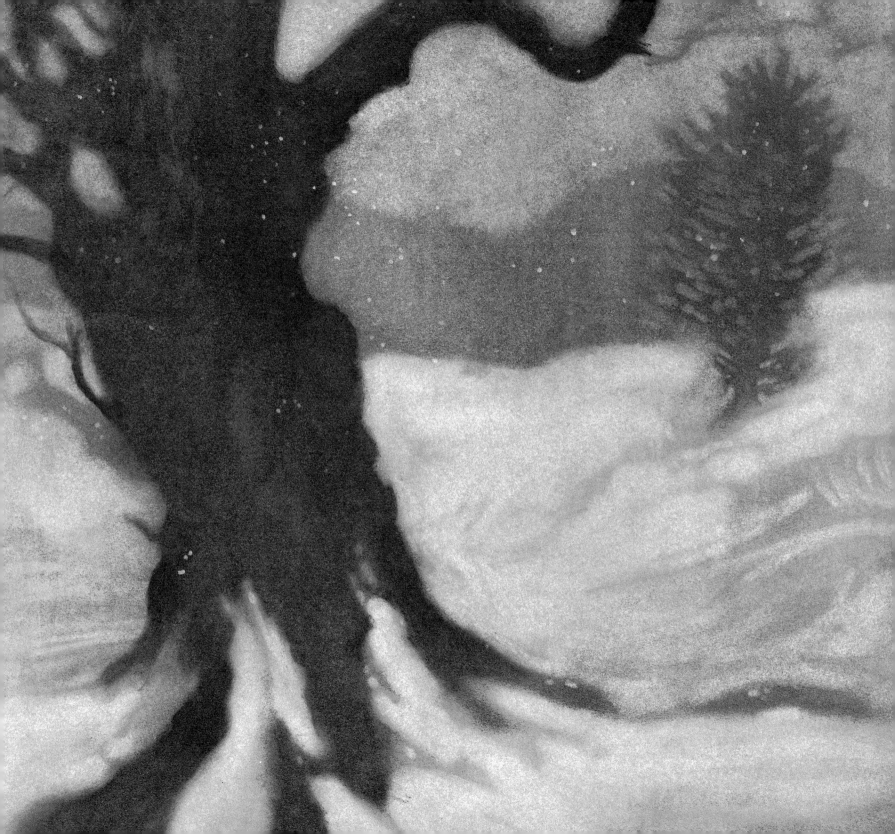

A Gingered January

Outside, ice covers the roof,
Snow quilts the ground
Inside the kitchen, Grandma says,
"This oven's right warm."
And we mix us up a gingerbread man

A bowl of molasses, a dipper of milk
A dash of butter, and flour like silk
Ginger and the hen's fattest egg
Vanilla extract, sprinkled nutmeg

At last I taste a bite or two
"He looks just like you,"
Grandma says, nodding her head
And I eat up all the gingered bread

February Hero

Lightning skates across the sky
Tornadoes follow thunder
Twisting twisters break through clouds
That scare me speechless

Daddy takes my hand as we dash home
I hear him firmly say,
"I'll be your refuge
   From the wind's cruel storm
   I'll be your shelter
   When you need a place to come."

The March King

They nicknamed me Royal Lion
For royalty they say
And when I play inside
My court is all I survey

I rule brooms and mops
I rule marbles, the Ping-Pong ball
I move all over the house
My kingdom is the hall

My sister, who won't mind me, says,
"I don't care what you do
   I have dominion over me
   You have dominion over you."

April Medicine

My mother's touch, so tender, so certain
Steadies me with healing hands
Hands that cool my brow when I perspire
And warm me when I shiver

My mother's hands already know
The temperature of my head
The weather of my heart
How do they know to be cool when I'm hot
And warm when I'm not?

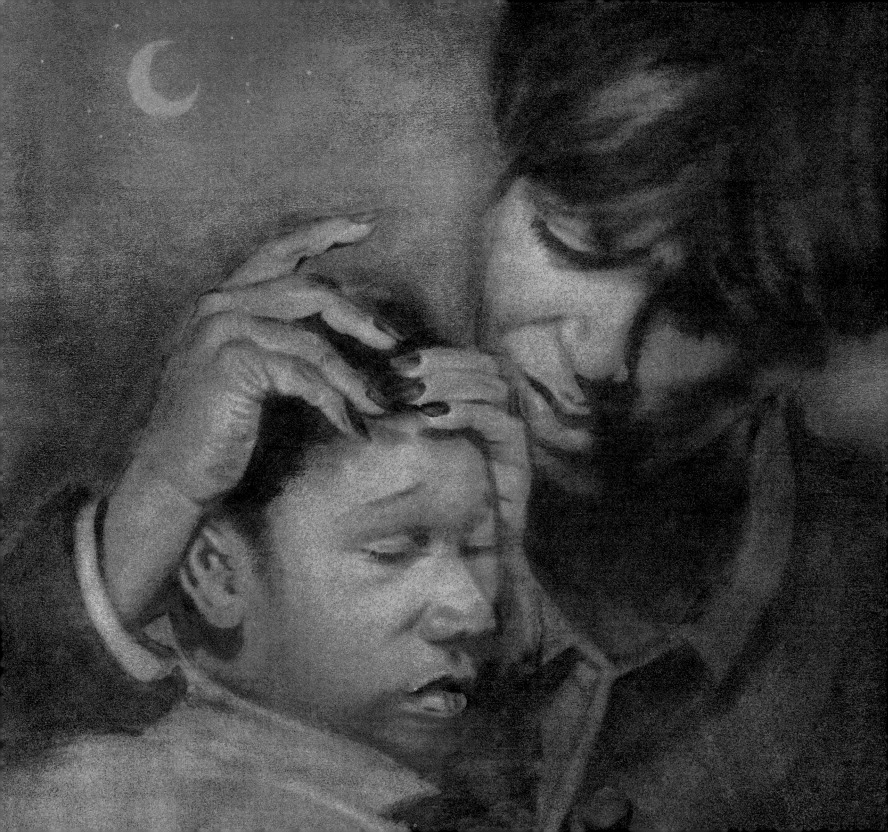

May Beginnings

"What's your favorite day in May?"
Mama asks, stirring the cake
She winks at Daddy as if she didn't know
"Today's his favorite," Daddy whispers low

And after that it gets better
Every day is sunny weather
As school days narrow
I hear crickets, the first spring sparrow

Imagine recess for months
And playmates for lunch
Friends camping overnight
It's my special day and everything's right

June Sunday

June Sunday I sit with my family
In a church of paneled wood
I have come to worship
And remember all that's good

I feel encouragement from each gaze
Sit up straight, look solemn
Sing praise

Crawdads in July

The crawdads in the creek are baiting
The baseball in the field is waiting
My roller skates aren't hesitating
My feet are agitating this July Fourth day

Baton twirlers strut in blue and white
Then fireworks fix the night with light
I move like a crawdad through the crowd
Quick, red-blooded, pioneer, proud

August Cowboy

I woke up at dawn and rode
Grandpa's horse 'til noon
Think I'll ride 'til I see the moon

"I can see the tiredness in your bones
   I know all about boys, my son
   Don't you know I used to be one?"

Grandpa spreads a pallet
Stitched with Buffalo Soldiers
For a bed
"Oklahoma cowboys," he says,
   "With a dark man at the head."

September Yearning

Daddy hands me a shirt of many blues
And I've polished my sturdy shoes
And Mama's pressed my overalls
For the very first day of school falls
        in September

I reach for new books
And read about old heroes
I compute numbers
I calculate zeros

Then pages of poems I memorize
And paint the pictures
Behind my eyes

October Love

At our house this morning
I make the bed
Mama sets the table
Daddy cooks the bread

My sister stirs oatmeal with cinnamon spices
I peel the oranges and part the slices

We drink love for breakfast
Can't you tell?
One glass makes you smile a lot
Two glasses, and you laugh for no good reason

November Letter to God

Dear God, who carves the pumpkin round,
    Who paints the oak tree gold
    Who sets the sky birds free
    Thank you for my family
    Thank you, God, for blessing me

December's Song

My daddy's washed his bricklayer hands
Red and muddy with mortar

Now he smells like houses
In their early stages

Like the fireplace
He's built and stoked with wood
As it flashes bright
Enough to warm my chilly bones

His chapped hands are brave
With work
Rough with knowing
How to keep a family from freezing
How to keep a young mind growing

He is a gift all by himself
His hands ungloved
His heat, his love

It's December
And of all the gifts December brings
I'll always remember
That people are more important than things

Gingerbread Days
stay a while in the warm seasons
of our fathers

DATE DUE

AUG 2 8 2007		
FEB 2 5 2019		
JAN 2 9 2019		
JAN 1 6 2020		

GAYLORD   #3523PI   Printed in USA